ACTIVE SPORTS Scuba Diving

Published by Creative Education

P.O. Box 227, Mankato, Minnesota 56002

Creative Education is an imprint of The Creative Company

www.thecreativecompany.us

Design by Blue Design

Production by The Design Lab

Printed in the United States of America

Photographs by Alamy (Alexander Caminada, Reinhard Dirscherl, David
Fleetham, Guillen Photography/USA/South Padre Island, WaterFrame),
Corbis (Bettmann, Stephen Frink), Getty Images (Stephen Frink, Zena
Holloway, Peter Pinnock), iStockphoto (Simon Gurney, Carri Keill, Cornelis
Opstal, Tammy Peluso, Bart Sadowski, Miguel Angelo Silva, Martin Strmiska,
Martin Strmko, Jose Tejo)

Library of Congress Cataloging-in-Publication Data

Bodden, Valerie.
Scuba diving / by Valerie Bodden.
p. cm. — (Active sports)
ISBN 978-1-58341-701-0
Includes index.
1. Scuba diving—Juvenile literature. I. Title.

GV838.672.B63 2009
797.2'3—dc22   2007051578

First Edition
9 8 7 6 5 4 3 2 1

Scuba Diving

Valerie Bodden

CREATIVE EDUCATION

Scuba divers can see coral reefs up-close.

Pretty fish swim around you. There is a bright **coral reef** below you. You kick your feet and swim through the water. Scuba diving shows you a whole new world!

Jacques Cousteau (middle)

Scuba divers swim far under the water. People cannot breathe underwater, though. Until about 60 years ago, divers had to breathe air from a hose. The hose went to a boat above the water. Then, two men named Jacques-Yves Cousteau (*zhahk eev koo-STOH*) and Emile Gagnan (*ay-MEEL GAHN-yahn*) **invented** scuba gear.

Some people hold their breath for short dives.

Scuba divers wear a tank full of air on their back. The divers breathe air from the tank through a hose. With the tank, divers can stay underwater for about 90 minutes.

Divers can sometimes go under thick ice.

Most scuba divers wear special diving suits called wet suits. The wet suits keep them warm. They wear long, flat shoes called flippers, too. The flippers help them swim faster.

New scuba divers have to be at least 12 years old. They have to take a class. In the class, they practice diving in a swimming pool. Then they can start diving in a lake or the **ocean**.

In some ocean places, divers swim with dolphins or whales!

Lots of people like to dive by coral reefs in the ocean. They like to see the animals that live there. Other divers like to search old ships that have sunk.

Some shipwreck divers find treasures such as gold coins!

Scuba divers have to be careful. They have to make sure they have enough air in their tanks. They cannot go up or down too fast in the water. Doing that could make them sick.

Scuba divers can go about 130 feet (40 m) underwater.

Scuba divers looking for sharks often stay in a cage.

Divers have to watch out for **dangerous** animals, too. Some sea snakes are poisonous. Jellyfish can sting. Most sharks will not hurt people. But sometimes sharks think people are food.

If divers run out of air, they share their buddy's air.

To stay safe, divers swim with a buddy. They use hand movements to "talk" to their buddy under the water. Thumbs-down means to go down. The divers can enjoy the underwater world together!

Some divers fix telephone lines under the water.

GLOSSARY

coral reef—a ridge in the ocean made from the hard, colorful outsides of tiny sea animals

dangerous—not safe

invented—made something new that had never been made before

ocean—a huge area of deep, salty water

poisonous—containing something that can make people sick or kill them